Reviews

"Wise, worldly and persuasive, these poems invite us to explore life's passages from a seaside childhood through untapped landscapes, heartache and bereavement, and hard-earned enlightenment. Delivered with clarity and assurance, the poems sweep us along until, with the poet, we can let the Earth sing. Careful attention to subtle occasional rhyming and unobtrusive assonance and alliteration contribute to a restrained, careful eloquence. Ultimately, we are urged, in sincere and passionate entreaties, to value and preserve our environment or face the consequences. Gill Foss knows how to lift the language and capture our attention and respect with seasoned skill and grace."—Sylvia Adams, Author of *Folding Laundry on Judgment Day* (forthcoming)

"In five distinct sections of her life, Gill Foss explores a full range of events and emotions with great understanding; she is never superficial. She shares her joy of international holiday travels, to her English childhood joys, to Canada's wondrous beauty of Lake Louise, to the forever emptiness after the death of her daughter, to railing at the lack of responses to soften climate change effects, and the amazing love that remains as warm as a first teenage experience. Arriving in Canada in 1970, she was soon winning recognition for her fine poems from 1978 from Alberta to Ontario in 2019 for her sonnets, haiku, ghazel and other poetic formats. Her fresh word choices and varying tempos or rhythms bring her lifetime of paying attention to detail as a gift to readers who enjoy good poems. *Personal Perspectives* by Gill Foss will give readers an urge to reread and quote her lines many times."—Bernice Lever, *Small Acts*, Black Moss Press, 2017.

Personal Perspectives

a collection of poems by Gill Foss

To all those who
have been part of this journey with me.

Table of Contents

Part Four: In Memoriam

Part Five: Let the Earth Sing

Foreword

This collection is a series of poems following my life in Canada as a new immigrant and the many aspects of my travels both here and abroad in Europe, the Caribbean, and Chile.

From my observations of nature and human experience, I have planned the collection as a journey in which family, love of the outdoors, divorce, tragedy, and rural life have combined to shape this newcomer into a Canadian citizen although, because of the threat of climate change, I have a guarded outlook for the future.

GF
2019

Part One

Past Times

Northumberland Childhood

The seasons of the sea were with me then.
I slept each night above its roar
carried the easy distance to my room
lulled through changing moods, until its
restless motion ceased to register.
Despite the years between, it haunts my dreams:
I feel an emptiness — the sea calls still.

Come spring when tides rode high,
we'd watch them crash against the concrete wall,
a towering arc of spray flung overhead.
We'd run beside the rails until,
misjudging some great giant, we'd land beneath!
Laughing and soaked we'd tumble out of range,
our daring paid for by stern reprimand.

On summer days the family would take
a tent and picnic to the beach so we could tunnel,
splash and race along the firm, gold sand,
or hire a boat and ride the swells.
When it was calm enough to watch the seabed change
from light to dark we'd see the rocks, sense under-tow
which yearly snatched a life or two.

In later days when solitude appealed,
I'd walk along the cliffs around the bay
to wile away my adolescent dreams.
The sea had all my passions, an understanding friend
whose company I'd seek. Sometimes with others,
shoes slung around our necks, I'd chase the little waves,
or sit and watch the fishing fleet set out.

St. Mary's Island marked the northern point —
before the port of Blyth smeared greasy smoke
and scribbled cranes across the sky. A lighthouse rose
above its rocks and little green-door'd cafes tempted us
to overstay our time until the tide sneaked in
behind our backs, to rush across the causeway.
Cut off, we'd dash barefoot through frigid swirls.

Then came November days when fog and mist
shrouded all view and crept about the house.
The sea was melancholy, echoed the flat, insistent sound
of fog-horns belling from the rocks which
once, despite those blasts, impaled a ship.
For years it crouched, a tilted landmark
pillaged clean and gaunt, defiant still.

My winter nights were audience to
the angry roar of restless waves
whipped to white horses or heaving like cresting hills
to beat with crashing force the walled beach walk.
Sometimes I'd watch reflections of the moon
chased by hungry clouds, elation rising with my drowsiness.
Now all I catch are echoes, as far away as youth.

Alberta Poetry Yearbook, 1978
Windows in Time, Beret Days Press, 2008

North Sea Fishing Fleet

I watched them chug across the bay, those boats
like painted tubs with netting strewn about their decks
stubbing their bows into each wave.

I sensed a strength, squat, butting power beyond their size
to fight the seas, gale-whipped with breaking crests
or heaving swell, like nausea

each with its crew of hardy men
who smelled of fish and brine and oil, with eyes
alert for sudden squalls in faces tanned by wind and spray.

Gulls wheeled and dived around the boats
like wind-tossed leaves in monochrome
flung between clouds and lively waves.

This recollection brings back memories
of fish and chips, and cockles in their paper cups
so long ago on Saturdays.

Windows in Time, Beret Days Press, 2008

Storm Riders

I sit and watch the seagulls
    like scraps of white paper against
        the lead grey sky, echoing
the upswept anger of the sea.
    Random they swirl,
      like troubled thoughts
throwing their haunting cat cries
        to the wind.

Windows in Time, Beret Days Press, 2008

Early Days

A lacy wave tickles the golden sand.
Red flags warn unwary swimmers.

Learning to swim in a seawater pool
I turn blue and shiver.

As I walk home with a new friend
we hold hands and smile.

Along the cliff path I pick wildflowers,
watch a turmoil of seagulls follow the fishing fleet.

On our winter windows salt speckles:
spray blown gale force from the North Sea.

Later I leave my youth behind.
Goodbyes are always difficult.

Windows in Time, Beret Days Press, 2008

Part Two

On the Move

Spain:

Flamenco Evening

(Costa Brava, 1982)

Lilting and powerful throbs the theme
of a haunting gypsy dance
played by a Spanish wanderer
to the bodega's empty stools.

A single dancer stands erect,
what poise and grace she shows
in a flounced red dress,
with hair flung loose
and a freedom in her eyes.

Slowly she starts to dance,
her clicking fingers raised
as the slender body moves.

With willow grace she sways
to the wildness of the call
as she answers to the pulse
that draws her ever on.

Soon the music's powerful spell
brings in watchers from the street.
First, they sit and listen
then they, too, feel the beat.

A single dark-haired stranger
glides up to join the girl,
they dance together urgently
to the guitar's strumming call.

Soon others join the two
until the rhythmic spell
has transformed all the watchers
into a throbbing whirl —
a mass of coloured movement
that seems to fill the room.

Yet still the gypsy plucks
a frenzy from his strings
'til the dancers reach a climax —
and the swirling tumult ends.

France:

Mont St-Michel — Normandy

Blue sands stretch out to meet the evening sky
which hazily enfolds this tiny isle
in dark relief.

Two listless row-boats lie
waiting the tide whose rushing course will set
sprays leaping round the gateway to the mount:
its town, clustered with concentration
tumbling on itself, seeming to flaunt
all possibility.

Almost
against belief, St-Michel Abbey stands
topping this crag, a grey and tranquil host
to wheeling gulls — God-proud with history.

Alberta Poetry Yearbook, 1984

Carcassonne

City
of artisans,
in Mediaeval times
fortified, invaded now by
tourists

Midi Camping

Flowers
grew through the sand
St Tropez, south of France,
on the nudist beach I only
bared breasts

British Virgin Islands:

Storm Warning

The scene, idyllic and serene, floats past
my shaded eyes while white sails billow, filled
by chasing breeze, like geometric clouds
across an open sky. Our engine stilled,

a brisker gust pulls at our jib. The swell
restless, small: now new-formed clouds ride on
the wind. I watch them grow as they foretell
a sudden weather change. A storm is born.

Reflecting the arousal of the wind,
the waves, white-crested now, race on their way
while darkening clouds blown round us from behind
eclipse with growing speed the once-wide sky.

Against the rising wind and broken sea
we beat for port, in tense expectancy.

Alberta Poetry Yearbook, 2nd Place, Sonnet category, 1979
Whistle for Jelly Fish, Bookland Press, 2011

A Window in Time

I plumb my mind to find the memory
of Caribbean nights beneath a sail
watching the stars. My shoulders draped
with soft, fringed shawl, pale blue
against brown arms, sun-soaked.
The moon reflected in a restless mirror.

Once home again, the scene was mirrored
in my mind, a porthole memory
to be recalled on dull days, soaked
with autumn sadness. Or when sales
of winter boots have left me waiting for the blue
of sun-filled skies and trees again green-draped.

I think once more of swimsuits draped
over the rails to dry — this vision mirrors
anew that image, azure blue,
as Wordsworth saw from memory
his daffodils. In retrospect I sail
through time, my mind dream-soaked.

While days were hot, rain soaked
the towels or new-washed clothes left draped
outside at night, but we'd not sail
until the sun caught tiny fish, like mirrors,
leaping in rainbows from the waves. A memory
of times long past, dimmed but no less blue.

Such thoughts as these have never left me blue
despite young friendships left behind. I soak
up images of firm, gold sand where memories
of beach-side bars, shade-draped
were formed to last forever — a mirror
in the mind, time can't assail.

Only in retrospect I'll sail
again those waters clear and blue
where minds reflect like mirrors
the corals bright with life and soaked
with dappled sunlight filtered through the drape
of dancing ripples, saved as memories.

These scenes are mirrors where I soak
dried thoughts, to sail again the blue
of times long-draped in memory.

Whistle for Jelly Fish, Bookland Press, 2011

Snorkelling above the *RMS Rhone*

I hover weightless
in the summer's gentle swell
above Tortola's silent rocks
that long ago impaled a ship whose crew
fought hard that day against wild odds
beyond experience.

This sunken hulk, the *RMS Rhone*,
lies broken, with the bones
of long-dead men,
now dappled with sun
and darting fish.

I sense the cries of fear
rise like the hurricane
that caused this tragedy
and wonder if those ghosts resent
becoming a tourist attraction.

Whistle for Jelly Fish, Bookland Press, 2011

Farewell to *Caribbean Zoe*

(For Sale at a Mississauga dock)

Moored
    fast to the dock
mast and boom
    write a sad semaphore,
hatches battened
    spattered with dried tears of salt rain,
companions padlocked
    against trespassers,
sheets & ropes
    tied in neat knots
hanging with memories
    like discarded skins.

Only remembering sees
    t-shirts drying in the wind
& children diving
    into a blue, blue sea
so clear the bottom winks
    an invitation
to flirt with sunbeams/
    search for secrets.
I grieve as she waits
    for someone else
to see new
    possibilities.

TOPS (The Ottawa Poetry Society), *Outward Bound Anthology*,
2004

Chile:

Valparaiso

City of hills where buildings tumble
row upon row towards the sea.
I slowly trudge up hills
breathless from winter sloth
stopping to gaze around
(a brief excuse to rest)
while soaking up the sights and smells
of outdoor cafes, trams and sea.

Neruda's *La Sabastiana*, perched atop a cliff, gazes
across the harbour, an eyrie for a poet
to drink with friends and speculate on politics
and love.

I scuff my way down roads
and broken sidewalks
past brightly painted doors, and windows
adorned by fancy grills that whisper "Spain",
and sleeping dogs.

Funiculars draw short parallels
on hillsides stitched together,
glass fronted rail cars give a fleeting view
over descending rooftops
of tiny gardens, balconies and everywhere
colour is rampant — alive, to match
the heat that rises at each step
beneath the blazing sun.

Whistle for Jelly Fish, Bookland Press, 2011

El Pueblito Los Dominicos

(Las Condes)

lapis
lazuli blue
earrings like chandeliers
showcased beneath the counter glass
tempt me

Los Parronales

poolside
we'd sit and chat
with avocado dip
and jugs of pisco sour until
sunset

Part Three

Oh Canada

Leaving England

(excerpt from "Fertile Ground")

Behind us the sun slides into memory:
like my last look at Wiltshire's Downs
as we left England on a virgin course.
I pulled my roots from native soil,
felt them trail vulnerable in rushing air
then with the tickle of expectancy
reach down to seek more fertile ground.

Whistle for Jelly Fish, Bookland Press, 2011

First Impressions on a Misty Morning

As if suspended between
the blue and green, I sit
amidst the golden mist of the waking lake
it enshrouds me
my mind floats in reverie
deep in the silence of this mystery.

I feel the radiance of dawn
bursting through summer leaves
and joy in the wild cries of the loon.

An ancient peace tides within me.
I am one with the earth and sky —
a spirit, free to transcend age and time.

I wade through sun-tipped ripples
to lie beneath the still dawn-cool of trees,
alone with wilderness and solitude.

Canoe at Sunset

A gentle evening, summer quiet,
a sunny lake and tent nearby.
The time and place for a canoe
that moves through water like a sigh
with no intrusion on the scene:
participation from outside.

The paddle zips a tiny wake
of drips that gather speed
then dips again with silent power
into the water, dark with weed
that gently laps beneath the boat:
the only sound to intervene.

Above, pink clouds blend into grey
as the sun's hypnotic eye
masters attention until dragged
by unseen forces from the sky.
Below, the dimpled waters blow
and knots of weed pass noiselessly.

An evening chill pervades the air.
Reluctantly we head for home.
A smudge of smoke against the trees
guides our new direction
to where, among those darkening trees,
campfires distil the setting sun.

Honourable Mention, National Capital Writing Contest, 2007
Whistle for Jelly Fish, Bookland Press, 2011

Dawn

Mist, like memory,
draws veils so
trees float
beside pools shimmering
with sunshine
and the world awakes
to the ancient call
of loons.

frosted grass
    at first sun, suddenly
        a field of stars

tinkling wind chimes
with each breeze
a new song

Lake Louise, Alberta

What beauty sets alight my Eastern eyes
on this first close-up of your Western land!

A lake, still edged with tinkling chimes now lies
teasing reality, too blue. My hand

cradles its fragile diamonds, finely cut
into fantastic miniatures by sun

June-hot. Some unseen artist's brush has put
lens-ready, wind designs which twin the run

of melting mountains wakened by the Spring.
We walk together round the shore and climb

up past the snow where avalanches ring
like shots, and trees are crystallized with rime.

I squeeze your hand. This grandeur, peak on peak
has said it all. There is no need to speak.

Alberta Poetry Yearbook, 1985

walking hand-in-hand
    for this instant
        fourteen again

missing a friend
	how well I remember
		our yesterdays

KADO broadsheet, Spring 2012

Summer Life of Light

sunlight
    veiled through gauze
        curtains
casts secret
    patterns
        painted by the breeze

morning light, noon light
    breathe incandescence
        into a dry world
waking slumberers
    in lakeside tents
        whispering secrets
          to butterflies

sun-warmed trees
    imbued with indolence
        shade nesting birds
          hide shadows

late afternoon
    that Midas time
        when all the world turns gold
before the tide of light
    ebbs to the west

twilight
    the time between
        when moths brush soft wings
against the gathering gloom
    and fireflies dance

starlight
    is for wondering
moonlight
    for dreams

candle light
    the flickering of desire
        he loves me/loves me not
  until the flame
        blows out

Spring Pulse contest, 2008

"Phantom"

The boat, hull painted black, was riding low
upon the water, shying at the waves —
a high-strung thoroughbred eager to race
before the playful breeze. Her stays the staves
to harmonize the music of the wind.
The sun danced sparkles on her spattered bow
while the white sail rose trembling, to be trimmed
once underway: the helmsman master now.

I felt her pent-up joy. When loosed at last
she caught the wind, cleaving the choppy lake
to droplets of protesting spray so fast
she left her rivals in a foaming wake.
Maybe I, too, should fly before the wind
and catch those fleeting words that tease my mind.

Albert Poetry Yearbook, 1981

Invisible

A spirit,
  I float on the wind
without shape,
    without form,
no more than an echo
   crying to the sun.

A shadow,
  I lie, concealed
without voice,
    without mind,
nothing but a secret
    whispered to the stars.

A woman,
  I haunt this life
without heart,
    without soul,
merely a hologram
    between two worlds.

Canadian Author & Bookman, 1982

Divorce

We grind each other
caught in our own spring breakup
hearts of jagged ice

Divorce strategy
a hungry maggot crawling
through my sanity

Legal jousting match
barbed spears pierce mailed emotions
delving for old sores

Affidavits sworn
motions propagate like weeds
seeds stored for Judgement Day

Cogs of Law mesh
mind fibres slowly stretching
Dead March to court drums

We study the board
to decipher their game plan
playing for checkmate!

Reflections

Dawn-tipped, the crags
scratch at the sky
while twinned reflections
etch their images
into the lake's
tranquility.

I see them as myself —
two opposites
in the mirror
of the morning.

Windows in Time, Beret Days Press, 2008

Canadian Authors Meet — 21st-Century style

(with unrepentant apologies to F. R. Scott)

No longer steeped in self-congratulation
Beneath a portrait of royal dignity
They do not see their monthly meeting's function
Tarred with old Miss Crochet's views of poetry.

It's true they stand in groups to share discussion
Not forgetting saintly intercourse, as when
They welcome unknown guests without delusion
Of grandeur, be they chaste, or old, or MEN!

Their air still heavy with Canadian topics
But no longer Lampman, Roberts, Campbell, Scott.
Today they're interested in publication
Though their subjects still require much earnest thought.

No longer cakes, it's cookies now and coffee
While they percolate their thoughts with the elite,
Exchanging tried experience and friendly
Market options, hints & tips, each time they meet.

Gone, the aimless, unimportant speculation
Shall we? Can't you? Won't he? or just plain "Maybe …"
It's technicalities & inspiration
And never mind that second cup of tea!

Oh Canada, Canadian Authors can
Ring out the knell for Scott's derisive image
With new-found strategies and action plans
To exorcise for good this dated outrage.

3rd place, TOPS (The Ottawa Poetry Society), B. O'Donnell Thyme
Poetry Contest, 2008

Staying on After the Conference

Left-overs
we wander through
empty rooms

elevators
with unfamiliar
conversations

and strange faces
other interests
whispering down corridors

only ghost voices
greet us now
in once-shared spaces

tomorrow
we too will become
invisible.

TOPS (The Ottawa Poetry Society), *Spirit Eyes and Fireflies Anthology*, 2011

Best Friends

(a ghazel)

A walk around Lake Louise began
a duet. Best friends for ever you said.

Eyes met and spoke without words,
togetherness in shared spaces.

Driving my Jeep along the cottage track
I remember when we walked this way together.

Later I watch the sun sink low
fading behind the cottage trees.

Do past times also lose their glow
as life and distance intervene?

When days are quiet and memories thrive
I still relive our interludes of intimacy.

Windows in Time, Beret Days Press, 2008

End of an Era

These past twelve years this cottage has been ours,
Has known the ghosts of all our joys and fears

As family members' dreams have come and gone
Guest house and cabin soon will stand alone

Already this plot's heart has slowed its beat
Once we move on, transfer this family seat

To smaller pastures, with a bungalow
Set on two acres, easier to mow

Than six fifty, almost a mile square —
Except it's pie-shaped — part treed, partly clear

Where we cut campsites for our summer friends
Who came to join the Meltdown crowd, a trend

That lasted half a decade. Music filled
The air and echoing round the lake spilled

Over the treetops, so our neighbours said
They could enjoy the bands while still in bed!

Bands once invited couldn't wait to come
Again the following year as my two sons

Set out to plan ahead their new program,
Repair the stage, enclose the new green room

Where waiting artists could arrange their gear,
Check amplifiers, speakers, without fear

Of interrupting those who played before
While quietly sorting out their proposed score

Each set would always run to overtime
The audience applause had just that aim —

To keep the music coming. Silent now
The campfire site is empty, wrapped in snow

Beside the lake it waits for summer fun
Of swimming parties, picnics, as the sun

Filters through pines above, encourages days
Of indolence. No longer will we gaze

Across the water, stretched on sun-warmed rocks
Watching the loons. These images will mock

The many memories we'll leave behind
Once all the documents For Sale are signed.

Ottawa Winter

The frost stings fire upon my cheek*
facing the bay at Andrew Haydon Park
where months before the flocks of geese took off,
determined lines of honking birds formed V's
instinctively to seek more southern climes.
Now I, on snowshoes, make a track towards
the lighthouse on the point, then turn around
towards the shelter, warmth and fire of home.

Later, when less frigid days move in
I'll take the Parkway down to Centretown,
passing spray-frosted trees along the way,
a fragile fantasy, the river's gift.
Then, warmly clad, with skates around my neck,
I'll join the fun of February's Winterlude.

*First line taken from poem by Archibald Lampman

Honourable Mention, *Poet's Pathway Contest Anthology*, 2019

Ode to Invisible Sounds

The fluttering of a falling leaf
or passing of a cloud across the sun.

An evening star winking in the dark,
a firefly flickering in the dusk.

A wish unspoken.

The smile of dandelions beside the road
or a turkey vulture rising on a thermal.

A crow swooping low between trees,
the taming of wayward ideas into a poem.

Steam rising from a cup of coffee
or the tantalizing smell of baking bread

To me, silence is the most invisible sound,
revealed only when it's broken.

Honourable Mention, National Capital Writing Contest, 2018

Rusticity

The crows caw conversations in dots and dashes
The old cat snores quietly in the rocking chair

The Midas sun touches each branch
I fall asleep on a hot afternoon to a chainsaw lullaby

Trees trimmed back in early spring
Hang heavy with a bumper crop

Red and green apples in the bowl — my own Still Life
Puffs of cloud steal blue from the sky

Shadows lengthen as the crows return
Sun-flecked dust motes dance to the whirr of fans

After rain the fireflies will light up the night
while Venus sparkles above a smiling moon

single leaf remains
last butterfly
of summer

against the evening blue
the tallest pine points
to Venus

62

fireflies
    unexpected kisses
        in the dark

Asahi Haikuist Network, July 2006

The Roost

Along with pine and spruce there is a tree
in my backyard, a chosen perch for crows
where raucous voices sound off-key.

At times it seems they squabble, disagree
first share a branch then swoop down low.
Along with pine and spruce there is a tree

whose height, a vantage point to see
surrounding vistas, flying to and fro
where raucous voices sound off-key.

Sometimes there may be ten until *ennui*
or a new interest ends the show.
Along with pine and spruce there is a tree

that dominates the landscape, makes a free
lookout for birds. When they're at roost I know
where raucous voices sound off-key.

These crows are fun to watch, I must agree
despite preferring birdsong sweet and low.
Along with pine and spruce there is a tree
where raucous voices sound off-key.

Bannister Anthology, 2017

The Act of Discovery

Pulling weeds, like digging
the meaning of words from
their context, separating the roots
as they lift from soil to land
in the basket of leftovers
waiting to be discarded.

    Once cleared, new plants
    are chosen: hydrangeas here,
    a clump of columbine, fall asters
    to keep the sub-context
    for the glow of a new poem.

The words their own colours,
each syllable freshly watered
into bloom — a flower of meaning
to be accepted as truth. Beside,
the wind-waving grasses edge
the bed like a fringed shawl
whispering, wondering
new interpretations.

    I wait impatiently to hear
    an explanation for the discarded
    images while I dip my trowel
    into the dictionary digging
    for meaningful discovery.

Honourable Mention, National Capital Writing Contest, 2015

uprooted last year
dandelions
trespass again

Haiku North American conference broadsheet

67

falling autumn leaves
echo the gentle patter
of morning rain

KADO broadsheet, 2015

Newfoundland Iceberg

My first sighting, magnificent,
mountainous, it could have been
a Lawren Harris painting, so white
and angular against a pewter sea

floating so serenely into the bay
its crevices secret blue shadows.
Captured on film, I can still feel
its cold breath on my cheek.

Judge's Choice, TOPS (The Ottawa Poetry Society), Ultra Short
Poem Competition, 2017

Bay Bulles Boat Tour

towering rugged cliffs
pairing birds on every ledge
no nesting for us

Haiku Canada Review

suddenly
in the rain barrel, my face
has no wrinkles

Fleeting Moments, 2011

in late sunlight
    lengthening shadows creep
    towards old age

Part Four

In Memoriam for Gwen

Thoughts on Upper Dwyer Hill Road

This evening, summer mist has reached across
the road, spreading its white shroud silently
into my troubled thoughts.

After her diagnosis, new today,
our futures will be filled with hope and tears
as treatment runs its course.

Her days 'til now revolved around
a family life with youngsters in demand,
alive with future dreams and plans.

What next? Hodgkin's Lymphoma,
an evil foe, needs strength and luck
to fight its creeping will.

Hope and support is all I can provide
in days to come, while fearing an emptiness
too great to contemplate.

Undertow

What good was Canute's threat
to still the raging sea
when tasked to play a god?

As each retreating wave sucks back
the shoreline sand to fuel
its next onslaught

so gradually lymphoma dragged
more life away
than spirit would admit.

As ineffective as Canute against the sea
support was all I had to give,
while watching her decline.

My anger and despair railed loud
against the undertow
that finally dragged down

a life too young
that left us weeping in its wake.

(Legend says King Canute demonstrated that his order for the sea
to quiet had no effect.)

Honourable Mention, National Capital Writing Contest, 2013

Sunset

The fragility of her life fluttered as
a falling leaf caught
in a shaft of sunlight.

She walked a tightrope
over the abyss without a safety net
balancing hope and denial.

Belief in trust leaves words unsaid
and all our little lamps of hope died down
the night she breathed her last.

The dead have found a way to float
into our mind's eye unannounced.
The dead are never quiet:

with dappled sunlight filtered through the drape
of memory I hear her still
whispering old dreams.

With our gathering to celebrate
her life, that day we said goodbye to
the last setting of her sun.

2nd Place, National Capital Writing Contest, 2017

Vacancy

A wisp of nothingness
the soundless passing
of a cloud
brushing away the daily
worries that itch
until they fade away.

Or a room without furniture
an empty space to make
a clean sweep with every
corner pristine,
waiting for input.

The emptiness of death
flows through my being
cleansing the pain of worry
and bringing acceptance
of the vacancy
she left behind.

TOPS (The Ottawa Poetry Society), *Transitory Tango Anthology*,
2017

In Memoriam

1967–2010

You passed so quietly from the light
too young to leave us that fall day
to grieve the early coming of your night.

You fought too hard to lose the fight
and yet lymphoma had its way:
you passed so quietly from the light.

Daughter, wife, mother all seemed right
and fitting for the sequence of your play.
We grieve the early coming of your night.

We watched your kindnesses take flight,
thinking of others all the way
you passed so quietly from the light.

You knew before the end your chance was slight
to beat the illness. We were left to pray,
to grieve the early coming of your night.

For nineteen months you kept the end in sight
yet never waivered, keeping death at bay.
You passed so quietly from the light.
We grieve the early coming of your night.

Judge's Choice, *Bannister Anthology*, 2018

Part Five

Let the Earth Sing

Changing Perspective

And this is why I sojourn here
Alone and palely loitering
Though the sedge is wither'd from the lake
And no birds sing.

     Keats: "La Belle Dame Sans Merci"

The changing season's creeping in
with golden leaves and autumn flowers.
Now hanging baskets droop and fade
as petals curl with cooler days.
Tomatoes ripen on the vine
and peppers turn from green to red where
market gardeners cull their crops
and birds fly south to warmer climes
while apple windfalls tempt the deer:
and this is why I sojourn here.

The sky is still September blue
while sun sinks low and shadows grow
across the lawn towards the trees
as years advance, approach old age.
Towards the elm at garden's end
a flock of crows come boistering
with raucous cries to evening roosts,
while I, beneath their noisy fray,
with leisured steps am sauntering
alone and palely loitering.

Some years ago I lived outside
the bounds of city lights
set in a half-tamed wilderness
of rock outcrops and silent space
where stags and does could roam at will.
From cottage door we'd take a track
down to the shore to fish and swim
followed by sandwiches and wine.
I'd go back now for memory's sake
though the sedge is wither'd from the lake.

I worry now with climate change
advancing faster then we knew,
if what I love of outdoor life
will still exist for those to come
as droughts or floods disrupt the way
we see our world while fierce storms fling
their devastation beyond bounds or
sun, no longer ozone-veiled, spreads pain.
Will all we hear be death knells ring
and no birds sing.

Judge's Choice, *Bannister Anthology*, 2013

Rothko's Dream: Ontario drought of 2012

based on #1953

"I am interested in expressing the big emotions: tragedy, ecstasy,
doom." — Mark Rothko

Look out the window at your lawn,
backyard meadow, nearby field.
What do you see?
A Rothko abstract, its yellow greens
transformed into a sere reality.

Light swathes of green, where shadows fall
to cut the blister of the sun, or patches of those
weeds not thirsting for the rain. His brighter
yellow, Lady's Slipper clumps, white strokes,
the dainty heads of Queen Anne's Lace,
unlike the centre of this field, a crisp expanse
of ochre stubble, crunching underfoot.

This painting looks a prophet's portent for a world
that left unrecognized the clues we should have seen —
a world of burning sun and wilting crops; sparse greenery
a wistful hope. Rothko perhaps saw truth. Who knows
what abstract inspiration seeps unbidden from a dream.
But here the artist's final swathe reverberates,
a wash of orange, offering no relief.

Honourable Mention, *Bannister Anthology*, 2015

Green Shift

The air is greening
with the calls of birds
shunning the long dark days
as winter wanes
eager to feel again the first
warm touch of spring
that speeds the weeping snow
to offer up the gift
of new life to the earth.

The air is greening
with the rise of sap
restoring life to every tree
as sprouting leaves bring
shade for hidden nests
from spatterings of rain
and flirting rays of sun
that hasten pleasure
with a lisping breeze.

The air is greening
with the insect wings
weaving among the trees
where beech leaves rustle
in the waking woods
the silent haunt of deer
after a winter's pall
when finding food was hard
and spotted fawns slept close.

The air is greening
now we have one more chance
to change our ways
before pollution and our greed
reduce our air to smog
productive land to desert
and foul our drinking water
with spills and acid rain.
Where will humanity be found
when we have killed the earth?

1st Place, National Capital Writing Contest, 2014

The Arrogance of Myopia

This earth — this ball of cosmic rock
millennia in the making now
threatened by the evolution
of Ape made Man.

We walk on the moon
create space craft to send back
photographs of nebulae
land on asteroids
congratulate ourselves on monumental
progress, laud our achievements while
polluting the rivers, land and seas.

Selfishness screens common sense
to erosion of the environment
for our future generations.
We look to the north for profit
not veneration for what it offers
to the life of man and beast.

What accusations at last will reflect
in the black eyes of a white bear
the faintest echo of a whale's song
or crumbling of a coral reef
unless we refuse to remain so blind.

TOPS (The Ottawa Poetry Society), *Transitory Tango Anthology,*
2017

Beyond HRV*

At first the odd events seemed strange,
mere sprinklings from a caster
until we recognized climate change.

Mudslides, floods widened the range
of antidotes that we should muster.
At first the odd events seemed strange

but then we started to exchange
our thinking, moving faster
until we recognized climate change

could be our fault, ours to arrange
a new approach that we must master.
At first the odd events seemed strange

before emissions which shortchange
life's quality, our next disaster,
until we recognized climate change

would need us all to rearrange
a joint approach to foreclose faster.
At first the odd events seemed strange
until we recognized climate change.

*HRV, Historic Range of Variability.

3rd Place, National Capital Writing Contest, 2018

Foresight

Today the gentle drift of falling leaves
as late September nudges into fall
set against a sky of scudding clouds belies
the climate threat advancing on us all.

How can we overlook the fact that change
is here, no longer can we put it off until
our politicians deem the time is right.

Give it some thought as glaciers melt to raise
the level of the sea until small islands
disappear beneath the waves. What then
their populations? Do we care?

———

The new food guide does not foresee
that many food stuffs too will disappear
as where they grow will be too hot or dry
to bring forth harvest, never mind the cost
of transportation that will make whatever still
remains too dear for most to buy.

What can we do as remedy? Each on his own
must make a lifestyle change. Drive less, grow
food on balconies/in yards, support a local
enterprise. Eat only seasonal fare that needs
no long haul transport, or container ships
to keep pollution levels down.

———

This means a backwards step that we are loath
to take. This earth's a precious gift, not to destroy
in heedless haste without a forward thought.

The powers that be must think again, take action
to preserve that which is left despite the kickback
from the corporate world, those who see profit
in every enterprise and damn the cost. Our children
and their children too are far too precious to ignore.

———

We must turn back the clock or change our ways.
Unless we do, what future do we have? At least
begin to plan ahead and bring some hope before
salvation is a spaceship to another world.

Honourable Mention, Spring Pulse Poetry Contest, 2019

Acknowledgements

I have many people to thank for help along the way in the preparation of this collection, in particular the past and present members of the Ottawa Field Stone Poets group for their constructive criticism and helpful comments over many years. My thanks also cover those members of the Canadian Authors Association and Haiku Canada whose input has been so important. I owe my special gratitude to Sherrill Wark who has been such a vital participant in the production of this book.

About the Author

Gill Foss has been writing poetry since coming to Canada in 1970 with husband and four young children. She is a long-time member of the Canadian Authors Association in which she has held many positions at both local and national levels. She is also a member of Haiku Canada, the Ontario Poetry Society, and Ottawa's Field Stone Poets. While she was writing feature articles for magazines, she belonged to the Periodical Writers Association of Canada.

Many of Gill's poems have placed in contests and been published in magazines. She has two chapbooks published, *Windows in Time* (2008) and *Fleeting Moments* (2011) and was one of ten poets featured in *Whistle for Jelly Fish,* published by Bookland Press (2011).

She now lives in rural Ottawa, which has added to her appreciation of country life. This is her first full-length manuscript.